Corporation Ethics

The Quest for Moral Authority

EDITORS

George W. Forell

William H. Lazareth

FORTRESS PRESS   PHILADELPHIA

Library of Congress Cataloging in Publication Data

Main entry under title:

Corporation ethics.

(Justice books)
Bibliography: p.
1. Business ethics—Addresses, essays,
lectures. 2. Industry—Social aspects—Addresses,
essays, lectures. I. Forell, George Wolfgang.
II. Lazareth, William Henry, 1928–
III. Series.
HF5387.C67   241'.644   79-8899
ISBN 0-8006-1556-5

8026K79   Printed in the United States of America   1–1556

Contents

Making Ethical Issues Part of Corporate Decision-Making

Christopher L. Davis *

INTRODUCTION

THE recent wave of disclosures of bribery and other illegal practices by large business corporations, coming on top of growing concern about such issues as environmental pollution, product safety, and discriminatory employment practices, has made many people involved in business corporations very conscious of the questions about whether and how corporations should take ethical considerations into account in making business decisions. For some time there has been substantial public debate on these issues, raging around the banner of "corporate social responsibility." Much of this debate has focused on the question of whether corporations should be "socially responsible" and should make ethical considerations a part of business and financial decisions. For those individuals in corporations who already believe that the ethical dimensions of their decisions about business matters should be considered explicitly and taken into account, the question of *how* to do this remains.

I do not believe that there is any single or readily applicable solution to this extremely difficult—although essential—task of making ethical issues a part of decision-making in business. Corporations are as varied as individuals in size, structure, spirit,

*The author is a graduate of Yale College and Law School and presently resident counsel with the Ford Foundation in New York City.

and the environment in which they live. Despite this variation, a
number of recurring problems appear when business executives
and their advisers begin to think and talk explicitly about the
ethical aspects of otherwise familiar business decisions. This essay
will describe three such recurring areas of difficulty and discuss
problems which are encountered and alternative approaches
which have been taken. These areas are (1) the problem of
making discussion of ethical issues legitimate, (2) the problem of
dealing with ethical principles and rules from different sources of
authority, and (3) the problem of weighing and integrating
ethical concerns with the economic, legal, and other factors that
are part of a business decision.

These problem areas are hardly unique to business corporations. For persons working in or with corporations it is helpful to be alert to these problems and how they may arise as corporate decision-makers begin to try to take these "new" factors
into account. It is important to keep in mind that while business
managers and their advisers are often expertly knowledgeable
about the facts relating to business decisions, few have any special
expertise or experience in ethical analysis, and most will feel they
are proceeding into relatively unexplored territory when ethical
issues are raised.

In this essay I will use the word *ethical* very broadly and will
not focus in detail on the nature of ethics and ethical issues. A
broad definition is necessary, because for many persons the
process of taking ethical issues into account begins with an understanding that closely resembles Webster's definition of
"ethics" as dealing with "what is good and bad and with moral
duty and obligation." The problems that this essay discusses arise
as people begin to work together to give this general definition
content and then apply it in the context of a particular work situation.

Much of the recent discussion of ethics and business practices
has arisen in connection with instances of bribery and other
questionable activities by large, "respectable" corporations. Such
instances hardly involve normal everyday business decisions and
are often like those critical times in the lives of individuals that

force us to stop "doing business as usual" and think more carefully about what is important—the implications of our actions and our values. Whether facing a demand for a bribe, trying to understand what caused some questionable payment in the past, or making a decision about a company's future policy, the business people concerned are frequently forced to realize that more than economic factors must be taken into account.

THE PROBLEM OF LEGITIMACY

The way in which business people in corporations discuss and make decisions in many cases has much structure and tradition. Persons working together in a firm involved in making decisions develop an understanding of what factors are appropriate to discuss and the accepted way to discuss them. We are all familiar with these often unspoken rules which govern much of what we say to whom, and how we say it. In the family setting it is common to find topics, such as sexuality, that are openly discussed in one household but undertaken with great reluctance and embarrassment in another. In the college setting, the hostile and confused faculty reactions to student demands for "relevant" courses are a reflection of the fact that students are raising a concern outside the understood and accepted rules for deciding what the content of courses should be.

Similarly, in corporations there are understandings about what kinds of issues are appropriate to raise in discussions about business decisions. Issues within this common understanding are legitimate to discuss openly; people are used to such issues and expect them to be raised. Thus, in reviewing the work of a sales agent, close attention is payed to the amount of business the agent has generated, the terms of the deals agreed upon, and the agent's commissions and costs. But issues that are not within this common understanding lack legitimacy, and to raise such an issue may evoke reactions ranging from surprise and confusion and puzzlement about the issue that has been raised, to embarrassment at what is perceived as a *faux pas*, to anger at the individual's poor judgment in bringing up such a time-wasting, irrelevant issue.

The result can be considerable hesitation on the part of some individuals about openly raising an ethical issue, and difficulty getting people to respond to or discuss such an issue when it is raised. In the example of the sales agent mentioned above, the size of the agent's commissions and costs is understood to be a legitimate issue to discuss and evaluate, but the issue of the agent using part of his sales commissions to bribe or unduly influence customers' employees has not been, in many cases, a legitimate subject for discussion. Thus, after the discovery that a sales agent has been paying bribes or engaging in other questionable practices, the managers involved may realize a need to go beyond heretofore accepted economic factors in evaluating the sales agent's actions. But it may still be difficult for them to go beyond the understood and legitimate boundaries of discussion they are used to. They will be unused to the new issues in this context, they will not know what responses to expect from each other as they discuss them, and they will lack the unifying common understanding that it is appropriate to raise these ethical issues in discussing sales policy.

Of course, people in other settings, even those settings in which ethics is a central context, experience these tensions too. For example, members of church congregations who have participated in groups discussing marriage and family life often experience some of the same feelings when people begin to talk about the situations of unmarried couples living together or single parents who choose to have children. For many people these are issues they have not previously discussed in a church setting; they are not sure how other members of the group will react when they express an opinion, and they are not sure whether they ought to be raising these issues or if they are even relevant to a discussion about marriage and family. As a result of all these anxieties, discussion of what may be a pressing concern may proceed haltingly or not at all.

The point is not the problems one may have thinking about difficult ethical issues by oneself, but rather the difficulty in bringing new issues into group discussions—especially into groups like those in business corporations that have established structures, specifically agreed upon purposes, and common un-derstandings about the sorts of things that should be taken into account in making decisions and formulating policy. This diffi-culty of "legitimacy" is not unique to the discussion of ethical issues in business settings, but in many corporate settings ethical issues *do* lack legitimacy. In such an environment it can be pain-ful to be a member of a group and feel the anxiety and embarrass-ment when one person begins to articulate feelings that there is something "wrong" with what has been going on or that perhaps a practice ought to be looked at in a new light.

As one would expect, the understandings and common rules concerning legitimate issues can vary tremendously from group to group. Resistance to ethical issues is not always found in cor-porate decision-making groups, nor is it always impossible to overcome. In talking with many business people about such acute problems as bribery, one finds not only a wide range of attitudes among people working for different corporations but also sub-stantial variations among groups of business people within a single company. One factor that makes a great difference is the quality of leadership a group has, particularly the willingness of the leader to signal clearly that discussion about ethical issues is acceptable and appropriate. It is not necessary for a leader to take a specific position on an issue to get across the message that there is an ethical dimension to a business decision which members of the group must focus on and take into account.

An example of such a signal occurred in a situation where a group of lawyers and managers was hastily assembled to respond to a request. Permission was needed to pay a substantial bribe to help a customer and his family escape from a country where their lives were in danger for political reasons. There were many issues to be discussed: Were the facts accurate and the family's lives really in danger? What were the business implications of paying such a bribe? Was the amount too large? What were the legal problems with making such a payment? Amid all these questions the discussion leader signalled the group that he thought that there were additional dimensions to be considered. Taking the legal problems as a starting point, he said, "As we talk about the law, I think that in addition to man's laws we also have to think about our obligations here under God's laws." This statement did not settle the issue, but it opened a discussion about the moral obligations of the corporation in this situation and of the managers involved in the decision.

The opposite signal can be given much more easily. In one group of lawyers and managers reviewing some of their company's recently uncovered questionable sales practices, the question arose as to what kind of policy the company should adopt with respect to bribery of customers' employees in foreign countries. Once again there was a broad range of issues on the table: Was such bribery against the law? Were bribes necessary to get business in foreign countries? Could the company compete if it did not pay bribes? How much did it cost? During the course of this discussion, one of the junior members of the group asked directly, "Don't you think that maybe it's just wrong to pay bribes, even if we can do it?" The response from a senior member of the group was an awkward clearing of the throat, a "Well . . . ," and a rapid transition back to the issue that had previously been under discussion. The signal was clear: this was not an appropriate issue for discussion. After a message like that, it takes a quite determined person to raise the issue again or to respond by picking up the point and bringing it back into the discussion.

In acute situations tinged with questions of illegality, such as those examples discussed above concerning bribery, it is easier for decision-makers to accept the idea that more than "normal" business considerations should be taken into account. But even in such situations it takes attentive and determined leadership to create an environment where the ethical concerns that participants have can be articulated and discussed. Without a dramatic setting, it can be much more difficult to promote discussion of ethical issues. In the context of normal business decision-making, the task of making ethical issues legitimate has to extend beyond overcoming restraints and inhibitions to discussion. It must extend to promoting an understanding that members of the group are affirmatively *expected* to consider and discuss ethical issues. An analogy can be made to the situation one encounters in the process of overcoming sex discrimination in hiring. The first step comes when people realize, confronted with an "exceptional woman," that she can do "a man's job." The second and more difficult step is the slower process of getting people to realize that men and women can do the same jobs. This process requires a change in the common understanding shared by the group. Bringing about such a change requires steady attention so that over time the persons involved become used to these issues, expect them to be raised, and come to include ethical issues in the range of factors which are understood as something a business person is supposed to focus on and take into account.

Providing ethical issues with legitimacy so that they can be articulated and discussed does not by itself ensure that such discussions will be productive. When such discussions are encouraged and begin to take place, a number of problems arise when managers begin to try to take ethical issues into account in decision-making.

THE PROBLEM OF DIFFERENT SOURCES OF AUTHORITY

When a group or an individual attempts to take ethical issues into account in making business decisions, dealing with ethical principles and rules from different sources of authority can be a recurring problem. In a business context there are usually at least three different sources of authority to which the persons involved will turn for guidance on ethical issues: (a) the laws of the various branches of the federal, state, and local governments; (b) individuals' personal ethical beliefs, which may be expressions of religious convictions or other beliefs; (c) certain rules or policies the corporation may have concerning ethical issues related to business practices. One can readily think of other sources of authority that can be important factors, such as standards of professional groups, public opinion, and the attitudes of fellow workers. The presence of multiple sources of authority creates confusion in trying to take each into account and in trying to find an orderly way to resolve conflicts between authorities. At this point, I will focus on the three main sources of authority mentioned above, because they play a substantial role in acute situations where people are initially attempting to incorporate ethical issues into decision-making.

It should surprise no one that law is viewed by many people as a source of moral authority. While the nature of law and its proper role as a source or expression of moral guidelines is the subject of voluminous jurisprudential debate, people clearly look to laws both as expressions of ethical principles and as a set of rules which persons and corporations have a moral duty to obey. Because many acute situations (such as the examples involving bribery) also involve serious legal issues, it is not unusual for people faced with such situations to be particularly aware of the law. It is important in trying to understand the role of law as a source of ethical guidance to recognize the different ways people react to legal rules. To avoid misunderstandings in discussions involving this complex area, it is useful for a person to be aware of several possible sources of confusion concerning the ethical authority of law.

Most people regard some laws as having more ethical authority than others. Thus many people who take criminal laws very seriously as a source of moral authority are less concerned about the ethical implications of the Internal Revenue Code and are quite unmoved by the spirit of the Uniform Commercial Code. In addition, people vary in how they regard the same law. These variations, while not surprising, are important to take into account because they can lead to quite different attitudes toward legal issues affecting a business decision. Such differences sometimes find expression, for example, in arguments over whether the company should abide by the "spirit" or the "letter" of the law. While such an argument may be cast in terms of a company's duty to "obey the law," it may actually be about whether the law in question is regarded as just an arbitrary convention like a traffic regulation or as an expression of a moral position, like laws against fraud or murder. Decisions about whether to take legal risks (risks that a course of action will be found to be a violation of a law) may appear to one person as a straightforward question of weighing the economic costs and benefits but may appear to be an entirely different kind of question to someone who views the law under discussion as a source of authority on an ethical issue. Thus, for example, in the highly technical area of securities law, there are a great number of statutes and regulations that describe what kind of information companies must disclose to their stockholders and the public. In a group of business persons and lawyers who are trying to decide whether a sensitive or unpleasant fact must be disclosed, it is often possible to find a clear split between (1) those who view these laws as expressing an ethical position about the positive value of full and honest disclosure and the moral responsibility of company officials to make such disclosure to the public and (2) those who do not regard public disclosure as an ethical issue and see these laws solely as technical requirements, where the goal is to avoid the cost and inconvenience of being harassed by the government or sued by a shareholder for failure to comply with the law.

Another issue which can arise and be a source of confusion in discussions about the nature and extent of a company's obligation to "obey the law" is the problem of distinguishing between arguments about the ethical authority of a particular law and expressions of a different kind of concern focused on a company's (or a person's) ethical obligation to obey laws generally, quite apart from whether a particular law is seen as having any ethical significance. Arguments that a company should obey a particular law because it has a general ethical duty to abide by the laws (sometimes one hears people express this by saying that a corporation should be a "good citizen") frequently sound quite similar to arguments that a particular law has special ethical force. It is useful to distinguish the two positions, however, since they reflect different concerns and have different consequences. An example of the difference in the two positions could be the public statement of a corporation president that the corporation and its employees are to comply with "the letter and the spirit" of a new and unusually burdensome law. In evaluating what this statement means in making day-to-day business decisions, it is important to distinguish whether what is being affirmed is the employees' obligation to comply with the specific provisions of the new law despite their inconvenience, or whether the employees are being directed to go beyond just technical compliance with the terms of the statute and accept the policy and ethical position embodied in the law as something the company will work to express in its day-to-day actions.

This shift in focus, from the law as a source of ethical rules to the belief that a corporation (or a person) has a moral obligation to obey laws generally, leads to the second major source of authority mentioned above: the personal ethical beliefs of the individuals who are participating in a business decision. A great deal has been written about the sources of individual personal ethical beliefs and how those beliefs are translated into action in a person's life. In the context of a corporation, where an individual is functioning as a business person participating in group business decisions, I want to focus attention on one particular difference many people feel, the difference between the application of their personal ethical beliefs in their nonbusiness life and the application of these beliefs in their actions on the job.

The existence of a separation between the ethical standards which are applicable to home as opposed to those that are applicable to business life is vividly illustrated by many of the cases of corporate illegality that have been disclosed over the past several years. It is not unusual to unravel a complex scheme of false records and hidden bribery and to discover that the business persons involved are generally otherwise honest and responsible persons who are quick to point out that all this was done not for their own benefit but to help their company. In fact, these business people are frequently not acting for their direct personal benefit, nor are they engaging in similar sorts of illegal or improper action in their nonbusiness life. The business person who bribes a purchasing agent to get an order for his or her company would be outraged if it were suggested that they improve their child's grades by bribing the teacher.

Such sharp differences in standards of behavior are often caused by strong feelings of duty and loyalty toward the company and by confusion about what that duty requires—that is, what place the individual's personal values have in relation to the duty of shaping and carrying out the business objectives of the corporation. Many business persons see themselves filling a role and performing a function that is directly related to achieving their corporation's economic objectives. In this role, a manager's personal ethical beliefs appear to be unrelated to the business objectives which are the manager's responsibility. They appear as idiosyncratic personal limitations on the ability of the business person to fulfill his or her business function. This problem is reinforced by the problem discussed earlier of the legitimacy of ethical issues as part of business decisions. The feeling that personal ethical values may limit a manager's ability to perform his or her duties is illustrated by the earlier discussion of using bribery as a tool of company policy. For some time there has been a vigorous public argument that because United States companies are prohibited from bribing foreign government officials, they will be unable to compete effectively for business in some parts of the world with foreign corporations that are not so limited. Proponents of this position believe that a prohibition against bribery—whether through law or through the personal convictions of individual managers—is a parochial restriction on United States-based corporations which interferes with the achievement of the corporation's objectives, as defined in economic terms.

One result of the uncertainty about the legitimacy of personal values in the business context is that people turn to alternative sources of individual ethical guidelines that are focused specifically on business problems and circumstances. For some professionals, such as lawyers, accountants, and doctors, formal systems of "professional ethics" are available. For other professional groups the equivalent of such systems may be found in informal but widely accepted industry customs, which form accepted standards of behavior. Such codes of ethical behavior—whether formal or informal—have two noteworthy attractions. First, they have greater legitimacy and acceptance in the business context among business and professional colleagues; second, they generally focus directly on the particular types of recurring situations which give rise to problems in a profession. This focus on the experiences common to one's own profession or trade is very helpful. It is not easy to identify in advance situations that may give rise to difficulties, much less think through the consequences of alternative courses of action. Professional ethics alert a public accountant, for example, in advance to situations that may compromise his or her independence and thus affect the accuracy and objectivity of the work. Likewise, the custom among professional traders in foreign currency of scrupulous adherence to oral commitments is a response to the critical need for personal honesty in an environment where tens of millions of dollars (as well as yen, Swiss francs, and Deutsche marks) must be bought and sold at a pace allowing the exchange of only a few words over the telephone.

Such often helpful focus on particular situations that may be unique to a profession or trade can also be a source of considerable confusion because it may obscure the basic values that underlie the guidelines. Because professional ethics are closely tied to the particular context of a profession and focus frequently on quite specific recommendations on how to act, the values that form the analysis of the facts and recommendations for action are not always clear and obvious. Consequently, individuals who carefully follow the ethical guidelines of their trade may never have examined the basic values those guidelines reflect and how those values relate to their own personal ethical beliefs. I do not mean to suggest here that attention to and reliance upon professional ethics and business custom necessarily imply either uncritical acceptance or the abandonment of one's own values. In dealing with a manager or professional who approaches the question of ethics in business in terms of professional ethics, however, it is important to be able to recognize both the benefits of such systems, particularly in identifying critical situations, and also the weaknesses, notably the possibility of substantial (and often unperceived) differences between the basic values of such systems and the individual's own personal beliefs.

Company policies addressing issues of ethics in business practices—the third major source of authority—have several similarities to codes of professional ethics and business customs.

Such policies generally arise out of the particular circumstances of a corporation and focus on situations that commonly give rise to serious or recurring problems. Such policies are also aimed at a group of people with a common body of experience, although in the case of company policies they arise from a common institution rather than from a common trade or profession. Company policies are different from the other sources of authority discussed above, however, because these policies are expressly designed to be an explicit factor in corporate business decisions and because they are an important vehicle for acknowledging other sources of authority and legitimizing their inclusion in business decision-making. Thus, in understanding and evaluating company policies related to ethics, it is useful to be aware of the types of issues such policies address and the basic approaches taken.

As a general matter, company policies often address two different types of problems. First, because such policies often are prompted by a company's troubles with specific situations, policies are often quite narrowly focused on rules about how employees should behave in such cases. Typical examples are the widespread policies regulating the receiving of gifts from suppliers and other business associates. This practice has frequently caused problems, and thus many companies permit their employees to accept gifts of nominal value only. As a result of unfortunate past experiences, it is not uncommon for certain companies to have policies that deal with more esoteric practices such as the use of numbered bank accounts or foreign sales agents. While such policies themselves may be outlined in detail, the values underlying such specific rules are frequently left unstated. Such rules have a strong "prudential" cast, however, and are often aimed at preventing interference with the corporation's economic objectives (such as might result from an employee biased by gifts from a supplier), avoiding violations of law and the consequent risk of prosecution, and describing specific business customs to which employees are expected to adhere. An unusual example of this last purpose can be found in the policies promulgated by several United States corporations in recent years which specifically address the circumstances under which bribery of foreign government employees is permitted. These policies attempt to spell out the difficult line between small tips and "grease payments" to minor functionaries, which the company views as an integral part of local business custom, and substantial bribes to government officials that both depart from business custom and result in serious violations of the law.

A second group of problems addressed by corporate policies on ethics concerns the sources of authority employees should turn to in resolving ethical issues in business and how employees should resolve conflicts between different sources of authority or between ethical concerns and business objectives. Policy statements that address these questions can be quite illuminating, because they sometimes indicate the attitude of a corporation's leaders toward ethical aspects of business decisions. Not surprisingly, many corporate policy statements are silent on these questions. Almost equally widespread are general instructions to the effect that in carrying out their duties employees are expected to follow the "highest ethical standards," without further elaboration. Such statements may often be empty window dressing, but they may also indicate an acknowledgment that there *are* ethical criteria which are relevant to business practices, even if the source for such criteria is left obscure.

A different approach can be found in policy statements which turn to the law as a source of authority. One multinational corporation simply stated that its business would be carried out in conformity with the laws of the countries in which it operated. This statement may appear at first blush unexceptionable, particularly for a United States company in the context of United States law. Its consequences become more readily apparent, however, in the context of a corporation which operates under a number of legal systems, including those of the nations of southern Africa. In such cases, a company's expectation that its employees look to the letter and perhaps the spirit of national laws in evaluating business decisions is a significant statement with which many people would take exception. Many business people find that conducting business in accordance with the letter—let alone the spirit—of apartheid is in basic conflict with their personal ethical values. A similar potential for conflict has been illustrated in the United States by statements made by corporations in the defense industry which seek to justify the production of such military products as napalm and other antipersonnel weapons. Such justifications cite national defense policy and existing legislation authorizing the government to purchase (or even compel production of) such weapons.

Corporation policy statements which directly address the issue of an individual's personal ethical values as a source of authority are less common, both because personal values frequently lack legitimacy in the business context and because there is uncertainty as to how to resolve conflicts between personal values and business objectives. The concern over these two issues is illustrated by policy statements which acknowledge the possibility that an employee might have ethical concerns about a business decision and advise the employee to discuss the matter with his or her superior. Personal values are recognized, but their status as a legitimate source of authority may be left ambiguous. A dramatic alternative to this is illustrated by a policy statement issued by one company that said it did not believe it could improve on the ethical guidance provided by the Bible and that it expected its employees to think about their work and act on the basis of their beliefs and in accordance with the dictates of their conscience. This approach both acknowledged the existence of individual values (in this case, specifically religious tradition) and explicitly affirmed their legitimacy in the business context. The company advised its employees that it *expected* them to include their personal values in their business decisions and to resolve any conflicts in favor of their values, that is, in accordance with their conscience.

THE PROBLEM OF INTEGRATING ETHICAL CONCERNS WITH OTHER FACTORS

Even when managers have overcome the problem of legitimacy and have come to terms with the various and conflicting sources of authority, there can still be substantial problems in integrating ethical concerns with the other economic and legal factors that shape business decisions. This section will discuss three problems that may arise as managers attempt explicitly to bring ethical factors into particular business decisions: (1) the difficulty of doing serious systematic ethical analysis, (2) the difficulties encountered in determining standards of business custom in the international context, and (3) the difficulty of putting ethical factors on a basis where they can be compared and weighed in common with other considerations.

The first problem is simply stated: It is quite difficult to analyze problems in ethical terms in a serious and systematic fashion. This difficulty might be trivial if it were not that it is both often unexpected and compounded by the fact that many business situations are different enough so that one's nonbusiness experience is not readily transferable. As already noted in the discussion of professional ethics and business customs, individual trades, professions, and even companies generate characteristic recurring situations which give rise to problems. Part of the utility of codes of professional ethics as well as company policies is that these characteristic situations are often both not obvious and quite complex. Thus, for example, company policies regulating payments to foreign citizens made in countries other than the recipient's home may alert company employees to a range of potential problems which can arise in this situation, such as complicity in currency control law violations and tax fraud. These recurring situations are frequently experiences which are not common in one's nonbusiness life and which can be very difficult to think through independently.

This difficulty is not unique to the ethical dimensions of business problems and is illustrated by the parallel situation in medicine. People have recognized for quite some time that medicine, both in normal practice and in research, gives rise to characteristic, recurring, and often highly dramatic situations involving ethical problems. Many topics, such as euthanasia and medical experimentation involving infants and children, are extremely complex and involve issues not common in many other professions. Like medical personnel, business persons may be intimately familiar with the factual issues with which they deal and may also be highly proficient at the technical skills of their profession, but they are rarely trained ethicists. In recent years many medical professionals have come to recognize that persons trained in ethics can make a valuable contribution to understanding those issues and suggesting courses of action. The relatively recent focus on bioethics as a special field and the increasing interest in and volume of literature in this area are testimony to the difficulties in analyzing these situations from an ethical perspective. These difficulties are understanding the often very technical facts, identifying the relevant ethical principles, and thinking through the consequences of different courses of action.

With respect to the ethical aspects of corporate business decisions, there has been much less comparable development. Business managers and their professional advisers have been slow to recognize that there are special skills and useful bodies of knowledge which can be brought to bear on ethical problems. A manager who would be appalled if someone suggested that any reasonable person of goodwill could do an adequate analysis of the financial aspects of a corporate decision is likely to be surprised and skeptical at the suggestion that these qualifications may not be sufficient for an adequate analysis of the ethical aspects of that decision.

Managers of United States companies who rely on business custom as an important source of authority for making business decisions in other countries may encounter a second problem: the difficulty of determining standards of business custom in the international context. It is often very hard to determine whether familiar United States business customs are shared in a foreign environment and, if not, what the local business customs are. It often appears that this question can be answered by a simple factual inquiry into local business practices. However, the guidelines for ethical business practices are not simply the range of business practices which are found in an industry, but a more limited set of practices recognized as the expected standards of behavior. In many business settings these normative business customs are unwritten and informal, although they may be widely understood throughout the trade. This informal quality can present substantial problems to a manager who as an "outsider" tries to distinguish business custom from the variety of observable business practices in a foreign environment. The task of determining local business custom can be quite difficult even when the task is recognized; where business people are not conscious of the distinction between "custom" and "common practice" which they make in their own cultural context, serious problems can arise.

This kind of confusion can be seen in the statements made by a number of companies defending substantial bribery of foreign government officials to obtain business. One argument which is frequently heard in defense of such bribes is that this is the way people do business in that country and that the company is following local business customs. When faced with a person making this argument, some further inquiry is required to establish whether the person is telling you that their observation is that bribery is a frequent occurrence in that country or that bribery is a practice which is an aspect of business life that participants approve of and affirmatively expect from each other. To get a sense of this difference in the United States context, consider what our reaction would be if a foreign car company stated that its policy was to instruct salespeople in its United States dealerships to use a variety of deceptive and manipulative sales techniques because it had observed that such practices as lying to customers and turning back odometers were frequent occurrences in the United States automobile sales business and had concluded that it should follow these local business customs. To us such a statement appears absurd, because in our own setting we can clearly distinguish between those practices which we view as the standard of behavior for car salespersons and the range of practices we may encounter. Thus, in the international context where a company relies on local business custom for guidance with respect to the ethical guidelines for decisions, careful attention must be paid to how a manager understands and has identified the business customs he or she brings to the analysis of the decision at hand.

The identification and analysis of ethical aspects of decisions do not complete the process of taking these factors into account in making business decisions. Ethical issues are one factor among many considerations relevant to a business decision, and to arrive at a course of action, a manager must consider the various factors in relation to one another and weigh their relative importance. This brings us to a third problem: the difficulty of putting ethical factors on a basis where they can be compared and weighed with other considerations. With respect to many factors, this weighing process is greatly aided by the business person's ability to use common economic terms to compare the relative costs and benefits of different factors. Thus, for example, in making decisions about a new product, various factors such as product design, manufacturing technique, advertising, and patterns of distribution can be evaluated in terms of their varying costs and benefits by comparing their effects on sales revenue and income. Although the factors relevant to a business decision may be very different, managers pay considerable attention to finding ways to make these factors comparable on a common basis using economic terms.

This presents a difficulty in the case of ethical factors, for even when it is possible to determine the economic effects of taking such factors into account, the "costs" and "benefits" associated with ethical issues cannot be completely expressed in or reduced to economic terms. In fact, for many people, to try to express ethical issues in terms of their costs and benefits (whether economic or not) may be to entirely miss the point of why such issues should be taken into account. Nonetheless, the difficulty in making ethical issues comparable to other factors can make it much harder to take these issues into account on a regular basis. Whereas many other factors can be systematically weighed in relation to one another, the manager is not able to use the same technique to judge the relative importance of the ethical aspects of a decision. In this situation, business people may with reason be uneasy when their normal techniques are not effective in dealing with ethical issues and they feel they are thrown back on intuitive "seat of the pants" judgments.

One result of this problem is a tendency to treat ethical issues not as one factor among many to be taken into account when formulating a decision but as a factor which is either not significant enough to affect a decision or so significant that it determines the decision. Thus, a business person who may be sensitive to ethical issues and able to recognize those critical situations where an ethical issue may indeed be the determinative factor, may not be able to figure out how to take ethical issues into account in the normal day-to-day decisions for which ethical issues may be relevant but not determinative. As a result, the ethical issues may simply be excluded from such decisions. This is important to keep in mind, because it suggests that in those cases where a practice of taking ethical concerns into account has begun in the context of an acute situation, where such concerns were of central importance, it may be unexpectedly difficult to simply "expand" this practice to the broad range of business decisions.

CONCLUSION

It is appropriate to repeat here what was said in the Introduction: I do not have any readily applicable solutions to suggest for the problems that have been described. There are, however, some general observations that can be made.

With respect to the problem of making ethical concerns legitimate issues for discussion and factors to be taken into account, I am persuaded that the quality of leadership and the degree of active commitment of a company's top management are central factors in changing the atmosphere and expectations inside the relatively closed environment of a business corporation. Of course, business decisions are made at all levels in a company, and I do not wish to suggest that ethical concerns should be exclusively (or even principally) the responsibility of the chief executive officer. What is necessary is an environment inside a firm where ethical issues are raised not at great risk by exceptional and courageous "whistle-blowers" but by ordinary business people in the course of their day-to-day work.

Institutional openness to ethical concerns, while it may be a necessary condition, is not sufficient in itself to assure an orderly discussion of ethical issues. The multiple and sometimes conflicting sources of authority to which individuals turn require careful attention to avoid substantial confusion. In addition to increased attention, however, there may be other ways to reduce the alienation from personal values that can occur in business settings. Outside the business context, individuals can turn to other groups such as family and church for support and affirmation. Likewise, organized groups such as churches, which are outside the corporate setting, can focus increased concern on providing individuals with such support. Within the corporation, statements by management and dissemination of formal policy statements can provide explicit guidance to employees on how to deal with this difficult area.

As efforts by business persons to take ethical issues into account expand, one can hope that there will also be increased attention to this area by persons skilled in ethical analysis. There are hopeful signs in the increasing concern focused on particular issues, such as United States business activity in South Africa, and more generally with respect to broader areas such as "socially responsible" investment activity and environmental concerns. Important as the attention given to such issues may be, however, they are just the visible tip of a vast iceberg of ordinary day-to-day business decisions. It is necessary to deal with the egregious and pressing issues, but our lives are for the most part shaped by the constant stream of "ordinary" issues. It is these day-to-day business decisions which are the lifeblood of a business corporation and for which it is most difficult to make ethical issues part of corporate decision-making.

Transnational Capital and the Illusion of Independence

Richard J. Niebanck *

THE term *independence* should be understood in two quite distinct ways. On the one hand, "independence" refers to the formal or juridical condition of state sovereignty. It denotes the recognition on the part of other nation states that a particular country is a member of the international community, a possessor of the status of "sovereign equality" with all other members. "Independence" in this sense implies that a country has been accorded, under international law, the full complement of rights and privileges of statehood, including the ability to engage in diplomacy, legal standing before international tribunals, and eligibility for membership in the United Nations and its related specialized agencies.

By way of contrast, the second, or "material," understanding of "independence" is at once much broader in scope and more dynamic in character. It is more the articulation of a good yet to be achieved than the declaration of a present condition. Rather than being couched in the formal terms of law and diplomacy, "independence" is understood in terms of power: the capacity of a country to determine the conditions and quality of its existence. So understood, "independence" takes in the full gamut of social, economic, political, and cultural realities constituting the existence of a people.

*The author is a Secretary for Social Concerns on the staff of the Department for Church and Society of the Division for Mission in North America, Lutheran Church in America.

Economic independence is generally recognized as a dominant subset under the rubric of national independence. It is understood minimally as that condition in which a country possesses relative autonomy in the disposition of its resources, the production of wealth, and the satisfaction of human needs under arrangements informed by a commitment to distributive justice.

Economic independence is seen as the absence of exploitive structures, whether imposed externally by a foreign power or interest, or internally by a privileged elite or class. It implies a decisive moving away from external ties of domination/dependency and an equally decisive movement toward the full integration of all sectors into an articulate national economy. In short, the idea of independence under its economic aspect requires the reversal of the present condition of domination from without and disconnectedness within.

The last two decades have borne out in countless ways how insubstantial juridical "independence" actually is. The granting of such independence by the former colonial powers has meant, for all practical purposes, the transfer of the governmental/administrative apparatus to an elite owing its existence to the metropolis. Furthermore, the ethos out of which this formal understanding of independence comes is one which masks vast imbalances of power under a putative equality before the law and in the marketplace. And the perpetuation of old relationships, albeit in new dress, with the former metropolis seems to have "frozen" any qualitative movement toward national independence as understood in the material sense.

One can identify seven features that are characteristic of the relationship between a newly independent state and the former metropolis:

1. The continued dominance of the local economy by foreign capital, and the consequent prevention of the breakup and restructuring of internal economic relations.
2. The continuation of strong political ties with the former metropolis.
3. The imposition of economic "cooperation" by the former metropolis.

4. The maintenance of strategic ties by means of military bases, arms transfer, etc.
5. The perpetuation of the old administrative apparatus by elites trained and selected by the metropolis.
6. The perpetuation of a common ideology.
7. The impact of legislative enactments of the former colonial power upon the economy and politics of the former colony.

The cumulative effect of all these characteristics is the perpetuation of a condition in the new country involving

1. Allocation/exploitation of resources by command (e.g., legislation, corporate decision) from the former metropolis.
2. An outflow of primary commodities (both nonrenewable and agricultural) for processing in the former metropolis.
3. Dependency by the new country on the metropolis center for technology, financing, and trained personnel.
4. Infrastructure (e.g., transportation, communications, market facilities) designed to facilitate outflow of primary commodities from the interior to foreign processors and thereby reinforcing the nonintegration of the country.
5. Minimal manufacturing for local consumption; most consumer goods imported to satisfy the tastes of the government and managerial elites.

The emergence of the transnational corporation (TNC) as a major form of the organization of capitalist production is the occasion for a wide-ranging reappraisal of "development" at both the conceptual level and the policy level. Seen by some as a potential benefactor (e.g., as an agent of technology transfer), the TNC is viewed by others as concentrated power without accountability.

Foreign investment can be an essential feature of Third World economic growth. The real questions are: What kind of investment? and, Who benefits? The problem is that present "hospitable" economic arrangements benefit the multinational corporations and the rich countries, but not necessarily the citizens of the poor countries.

The International Monetary Fund stabilization program, for example, tends to curtail meaningful technological and economic development. The tightening of bank credit makes it more difficult to obtain loans to carry on operations. Devaluation raises the costs in local currency of all imports and of all unpaid debts. This tends to cause economic depression, and results in the takeover of domestically owned businesses by their foreign competitors. Hence the transfer of resources within the poor countries from domestic to foreign ownership. In addition, devaluation raises the local price of essential imported commodities and the price of local products. Consequently, consumption is curtailed in order to free resources for export. The strongest local supporters of such policies are small groups of Third World elite exporters whose profits rise if the currency is devalued. Hence, the transfer of resources from the desperate to the privileged.

One result of this global mode of capitalist organization is the ability to permit and even to encourage the development of a certain level of manufacturing in the less developed countries. Based upon the "product life-cycle theory," this departure from the earlier colonial/neocolonial pattern involves the shifting of certain manufacturing to the less developed countries while having the developed countries specialize in production involving high levels of sophistication and cost (e.g., research and development, new technology, communication). The conflict that this shift sets in motion within the developed countries between the TNCs on the one hand and "old" capital and organized labor on the other is well-known. Witness the advertisements of the International Ladies' Garment Workers Union. Such is the power and flexibility of the TNC to take "the long view" and to act upon it. But it must be noted that such shifts of production, however dramatic, do not alter the basic world hierarchy of economic power.

As long as the rich countries view attempts at economic reform as a threat to turn the terms of trade against them, the prospects

for international justice as well as international political stability
remain precarious. In the light of such factors as international
oligopoly, the question remains as to how realistic it is to posit
"economic independence" as a goal that is achievable in more
than a minimal sense.

Recent Literature

George H. Brand *

THE MEGACORPORATION IN AMERICAN SOCIETY: THE
SCOPE OF CORPORATE POWER
*by Phillip I. Blumberg. Englewood Cliffs, N.J.: Prentice-Hall,
Inc., 1975; 188 pp.; $5.95.*

The author, dean of the University of Connecticut School of Law
and former president of a New York stock-exchange-listed
company, provides an empirical analysis of the dimensions of
corporate power in America. Blumberg finds that the large
corporations dominate the national economy and have a
powerful effect on the world economy. Of special concern is the
growing concentration of share ownership in the hands of
financial institutions. In addition, these dominant industrial and
financial institutions are governed by overlapping boards of
directors who share similar backgrounds, values, and affiliations.
Management is seen as a self-elected, self-perpetuating elite,
resulting in annual meetings that are mostly ceremonial.

Blumberg offers the interesting observation that the inability of
business to articulate its objectives in a way that commands broad
public support is leading to an erosion of confidence in the corporation as an institution. At a time when profit maximization is
no longer sufficient as the overriding goal of the corporation, the
business community must search for an ideology that embraces
social responsibility.

*The author is a research associate on the staff of the Department for Church and
Society of the Division for Mission in North America, Lutheran Church in
America.

CORPORATE SOCIAL POLICY: SELECTIONS FROM BUSI-
NESS AND SOCIETY REVIEW
*edited by Robert L. Heilbroner and Paul London. Addison-
Wesley Publishing Company, 1975; 347 pp.; $7.95.*

The selections of readings in this volume offer a significant cross
section of opinion on the structure and role of the modern corporation and its relation to issues of social responsibility.
Economists, financial analysts, editors of major journals,
political scientists, and business consultants view corporate social
policy from the perspective of their particular expertise and social
philosophy. As one might expect, the input of so many authors
provides the reader with a wide variety of analyses and opinions.
This makes the book all the more informative. The arguments of
the authors are on a consistently high level, and the essays achieve
a meaningful balance between factual data and conceptual
analysis.

Such issues as corporate concentration, environmental
protection, advertising waste, the social impact of technology,
the implementation of corporate social action, and the multinational corporation are given careful scrutiny.

The epilogue includes a thought-provoking discussion on the
future of capitalism. Do we still need the organizing principle of
the profit motive for the production enterprises? Can the
capitalist system solve the problems of environmental preser-
vation and of consumer protection? Can one expect meaningful
reforms in the distribution of income and wealth? Or does the
tendency of the capitalist system to generate more power to
produce than to consume imply a constant threat of stagnation?
These are important questions that demand answers.

LOBBYING THE CORPORATION: CITIZEN CHALLENGES
TO BUSINESS AUTHORITY
*by David Vogel. New York: Basic Books, Inc., Publishers, 1978;
270 pp.; $14.95.*

In this original, well-documented, and highly informative study,
David Vogel provides a detailed chronicle of the attempts of

numerous "citizens lobbies" to influence corporate policies in the direction of social-justice concerns. The author describes in great detail how class-action lawsuits and shareholder resolutions were utilized to confront such corporate giants as Eastman Kodak, Dow Chemical, and General Motors. Financial investments in South Africa, the acceptance of military contracts, industrial environmental pollution, and corporate hiring practices have become prime targets of these "citizens lobbies."

As a result of citizen pressure, management has become more sensitive to the notion of corporate citizenship and to the whole area of corporate social responsibility. In addition, these citizens groups were instrumental in motivating increased government regulation, which proved beneficial to the American consumer.

In analyzing the objectives of the corporate accountability movement, Vogel points to the "modesty of its demands on business." He writes that corporations could yield to practically every demand without endangering either their profits or their power. In other words, the nature of corporate power in America has not been seriously challenged by the corporate accountability movement. Nevertheless, policy decisions previously reached behind closed doors and insulated from examination and challenge have now been thrust into a wider public arena. And that, at least, is a beginning.

THE LIMITS OF CORPORATE RESPONSIBILITY
by Neil W. Chamberlain. New York: Basic Books, Inc., Publishers, 1973; 236 pp.; $10.00.

In this book, Neil Chamberlain, a professor at the Graduate School of Business of Columbia University, offers a sobering analysis of the inability of modern corporations to resolve the basic social needs of our society. In the fields of consumer protection, environmental control, urban renewal, and other areas of social concern, the corporations are unable to undertake the necessary programs.

Although the prospering corporation can exercise a certain degree of social consciousness in its planning, every corporation, argues Chamberlain, is limited by two constraints. First, it must show a profit that compares favorably with the profits of other major corporations. Second, a corporation must maintain a certain size and level of growth that enables it to continue in its basic activities. This corporate emphasis on profit and size are rooted in the very conditions of a competitive market economy.

Chamberlain clearly expresses what many writers on corporate social responsibility tend to overlook, namely, the extent to which social values and corporate interests are in harmony. The American economy is anchored in corporate society. As long as national prosperity depends on corporate prosperity, as long as the welfare of jobholders, stockholders, and consumers is pegged to the fortunes of the large corporations, most members of American society will continue to identify their interests with the interests of these corporations.

Any challenge to corporate policies will therefore be moderate and not endanger those operations which are basic to the corporations' economic viability. In order to find solutions to our pressing social problems, the author concludes, we will have to look to institutions other than the corporation.

"Ethical Guidance Provided by the Bible"—Confusion, Chimera, or Prophetic Realism?

Foster R. McCurley and John H. P. Reumann *

A PERSON of biblical mentality and outlook from, say, the period when kings ruled in Israel or from a small Christian community, like Corinth in Paul's day, would look with a certain puzzled wonderment upon the way we wrestle with making ethical factors part of the decision-making process in our large, modern-day business corporations.

This "biblical person" would probably not boggle at a broad sense of "ethical," even though the biblical mind preferred to think in specifics. "What is good and bad or right and wrong . . . moral duty and obligation" (Webster's third edition, unabridged) would be satisfactory terms. Even the notion of what was "professionally right and fitting" enters at times into the world of the Bible through the Wisdom tradition, for example, with regard to physicians and apothecaries (Ecclesiasticus 38), not to mention ethics for soldiers and tax collectors in the preaching of John the Baptist (Luke 3:12–14) or concerns over merchants and tradesmen and their practices (cf. Prov. 20:7–17; James 4:13–5:6; Rev. 18:1–8). If anything, our *homo biblicus* would insist even more on "values" and "the will of the Lord" than we do.

The puzzlement of biblical women and men, however, would be, on the one hand, with the enormity of our modern business

---

*The authors serve as professors of the Old and New Testaments at the Lutheran Theological Seminary in Philadelphia.

corporations, often multinational, functioning beyond sovereign nations as states of their own. Our finance and banking methods, our economic interlockings—so that what a cartel does affects the price of staples for the poor in Jersey City, Genoa, and Bombay, and profligate use of oil shapes national destinies in the Middle East or Mexico—and the complexity and speed of our business procedures would leave the ancients in awe.

Yet we must not overdo such differences, for Israelites knew of business links that went beyond national borders. There was export-import commerce, royal enterprises and monopolies, and great caravans traversing vast deserts, linking Africa and Egypt with the lands of the Fertile Crescent and beyond. Caravansaries, or khans, were places where cargoes, people, and ideas met. The "little man," the average "person on the street," must have felt helpless, then as now, before gargantuan economic forces and the power of the rich.

The New Testament world exhibits reflections of the huge tax-syndicates in Rome and the *latifundia*, or estates of absentee landowners, in Galilee. We meet in Jesus' parables petit bourgeois reflections of this socioeconomic structure in the "publicans" and household managers of "big business" enterprise. Jewish bankers in Alexandria, we know, got early news through connections of their own so as to shift sides expeditiously in the changes after Julius Caesar's death. Crassus's wealth was proverbial, partially amassed through tax-farming concessions in Asia Minor. Some commentators have thought that the high prices for wheat and barley mentioned in Rev. 6:6 stemmed from an edict by Domitian, regulating what should and should not be planted.

On the other hand, anyone with the outlook of Scripture would show even more amazement at our dilemma over whether corporations should be "socially responsible" and to what extent it is legitimate for them to take ethical factors into consideration in arriving at business decisions. To such a person, "the will of Yahweh" or "what the Lord has revealed in Jesus Christ" would be crystal clear in its demand that *all* of life belongs under God's rule and that God has shown how he demands justice, concern for others, and even mercy, in all we do. Has not God spoken and declared what he desires? The rich, the kings, the traders—everyone in business—all are under his judgment.

To separate from "personal ethics" any autonomous area of "business life" where God does not rule would be unthinkable in biblical theology. If we today look on the corporation as an "impersonal entity," the New Testament would doubtless vest it with a personality and personify it as one of the *principles* or "principalities" let loose in the world, and not simply as a "thing," as one of the *principia* (neuter). It is persons who make corporations go, and they each bear some responsibility.

Indeed, the relationship of the individuals to the larger group of which they are members is a key to understanding biblical anthropology. The so-called "Hebrew conception of corporate personality" (put forth by H. Wheeler Robinson) speaks directly to the relationship of individual and corporate ethics. In Joshua 7 is told the story of the defeat of the Israelites at the hand of the city of Ai—all because one man kept for himself the booty of a holy war which was to be given to the Lord (see Deut. 7:25–26). The means of identifying the guilty man demonstrates the corporate nature of the act: all Israel is to be collected, tribe by tribe, clan by clan, family by family, man by man. The lot finally fell upon Achan, the son of Carmi of the clan of Zabdi of the tribe of Judah. Because of the decision of one man, the entire community suffered disaster, and then corporately "all the people of Israel" stoned Achan and his possessions, including his children. It was a matter of individual ethics, but the results were corporate, because the community and the individual are here so closely related that the action of one incurs guilt on all. In the same manner, the solidarity of the whole human race in the rebellion of Adam and Eve can be understood.

The fluidity between the many and the one is attested also in the later structure of the community of Israel. With the establishment of a monarchy under a dynasty, the people of Israel experienced a new form of corporate personality. The king of Davidic descent was considered to be "the son of God" by an adoptive arrangement which took place on coronation day (Ps. 2:7; cf. 2 Sam. 7:14; Ps. 89:26–27). Yet the people of Israel too was considered to be "the son of God" on the basis of the deliverance from Egypt (Exod. 4:22; Hos. 11:1; cf. Jer. 31:9). These were not two different children but one son, the people, who was represented before the Lord in the body and function of the king. The royal decisions, the ethics of the king, were the ethical decisions of the corporate people of God, and so the results of blessing and curse were experienced by the whole nation.

As Robinson described the concept of corporate personality, he listed as the first aspect "the unity of its extension both into the past and into the future." To put it another way, the community is not limited to the present generation but includes ancestors and descendants. By this understanding we can interpret the word spoken by Amos in the eighth century B.C.: "Hear this word that the Lord has spoken against you, O people of Israel, against the whole family which I brought up out of the land of Egypt" (Amos 3:1). The community of Amos's day is the same community which had experienced the Exodus five centuries earlier.

In our own day the extension into the past and into the future of the results of corporate decision-making are all too obvious. The decisions made by our forefathers as the industrial revolution took shape affect the soil, air, and water in our generation. Likewise, the decisions of contemporary executives to sell baby formula in underdeveloped nations to undernourished people living in unsanitary conditions can have serious effects on the future generation. Thus the community to which our corporate decisions brings blessings or curses is not only international but almost limitless in time. It may be then that—without resorting to the execution of the guilty party, as in the case of Achan—the whole community must somehow hold accountable those persons whose corporate decisions affect all forms of created life both in the present and in the future.

Of course, here again we must not make too idyllic the picture we have of life in biblical times, for many an Israelite must have felt vast areas of life were exempt from Yahweh's gaze or, of certain practices, that "everyone does it," or "the king promotes such habits," or "it's legal in Babylon," and "Canaanites allow it." At Corinth there were those who would remove their sex practices (1 Corinthians 5) or legal relationships (1 Corinthians 6) or aspects of socioeconomic life (1 Corinthians 8, 10) from the sphere of Christ's lordship. Moreover, early Christians were not part of the "structures" in Judaism or the Empire. Their sense of an imminent End militated against involvement in such issues. And the minority and individualist nature of the Christian community (persons out of "every nation, tribe, and tongue" but not whole nations or economic guilds or syndicates) isolated them from any pretense of a "Christian society." The world then, as today, was one where people bade Jesus "to depart from their neighborhood."

FROM SINAI'S HEIGHTS, THE LAW . . . DEEPENED BY JESUS THE LORD

These words are being written after a climb to the top of Gebel Musa, the Mount of Moses, traditional site for the giving of the Ten Commandments, near St. Catherine's monastery in the Sinai. Whatever one thinks of the tradition about location, one cannot help but be impressed by the rugged grandeur of the spot, and more so by the moral demands in the imperatives from the God who had led Israel out of bondage in Egypt. Yahweh has spoken. People know what he desires. And the whole system of Torah was designed, at its best, to amplify and apply the will of God to specific human problem areas, to bring life into con- formity with that will. Sinai symbolizes the biblical conviction that God is not indifferent to any area of our activity, corporate as well as personal, and seeks the old values of honesty, uprightness, and fairness, to be applied in what we do together in his world.

In the present context of the Pentateuch, the Sinai law includes a number of law codes originating from different locales and times in Israel's life. All together these codes—as the word of the Lord to the people redeemed from Egypt—speak to virtually every area of life. The classic decalogue itself, Exod. 20:1–17, was all-encompassing for its day. According to a study by Hartmut Gese, decalogues in the Old Testament should be understood in terms of five pairs rather than as ten isolated imperatives. By transposing the commandments concerning killing (Exod. 20:13) and adultery (20:14)—on the basis of strong textual evidence— Gese sees the decalogue as treating the following five areas of life:

1. God, his exclusiveness and personalness (20:3, 4–6)
2. Cult and Sabbath, representing the realm of holiness in which humans can participate (20:7, 8–11)
3. Family, the sphere from which people descend (20:12, 14)
4. Humanness, the free life of people (20:13, 15)
5. Social life, the protection of fellow citizens, their rights and property (20:16–17)

This structure demonstrates a comprehensive system for human responsibility which extends from God himself to the fellow citizen. This divine concern for the totality of life, Gese explains, is accomplished by the Semitic device of speaking of the whole by listing parallel or paired ideas. Each pair of laws attests to the completeness of a particular concern, and the fivefold range of concerns omits no area of human relationships and responsibilities.

Continuing that same concern for the totality of life, the Sinai law includes the Book of the Covenant (Exod. 20:22–23:33), many cultic laws, and the so-called Holiness Code (Leviticus 17–26). The Book of the Covenant treats many specifics regarding worship and cult, slavery and freedom, bodily injury, personal property, protection of the poor and needy, court cases, and the like. The Holiness Code extols the holiness of God as the indicatives out of which ensues the divine imperative regarding such specifics as sexual abominations, food for the hungry, justice, restoration of property, and freedom. Contained in this code is the well-known imperative "You shall love your neighbor as yourself" (Lev. 19:18), a command which was regarded by Jesus as the second great commandment (Mark 12:31 and par.) and by Paul as the fulfillment of the whole law (Gal. 5:14).

Contemporary interpreters should not deceive themselves into thinking that the law of love is limited to "the neighbor," that is, a brother or sister in the faith, for in the same chapter of Leviticus occurs the necessary corrective to such a limitation: "The stranger who sojourns with you shall be to you as the native among you, and you shall love him as yourself; for you were strangers in the land of Egypt: I am the Lord your God" (Lev. 19:34). Christians know too what it means to be strangers and exiles in the world (1 Pet. 2:11; cf. 1 Pet. 1:1; James 1:1; Gal. 4:26; Heb. 11:13, 16), and so Christian individuals who participate in corporate decision-making can affect God's care for the neighbor and the stranger by seeking justice and fairness for all.

As is well-known, Jesus' teaching deepened, radicalized, and at points corrected "what was said of old" (Matt. 5:21–48). Though he did not apply God's will to any of the ethical questions of his day on a corporate scale, it is in the spirit of biblical thought as a whole for us to view God's will, for justice, as incumbent on all persons (who one day face a judgment of what they have done; Matthew 25, the sheep and goats[1]). This will for justice and morality is especially incumbent on Christians.

THE PROPHETIC VOICE

That Israel's prophets were spokespersons for God's will in matters of international politics and on social and economic issues has long been recognized. In particular, the prophet Isaiah stands out as one whose preaching abounds in political realities. Gerhard von Rad has shown that for Isaiah the real significance of the divine law lies in broad political contexts. This emphasis holds true not only for this prophet's preaching about the restored city of God and the rule of his anointed king but also in a number of utterances regarding national life. It was this prophet, for example, who was concerned about the forms of government which are appropriate to a society founded by the Lord, and also

---

1. See *Population Perils*, ed. George W. Forell and William H. Lazareth, Justice Books (Philadelphia: Fortress Press, 1979), pp. 26–30.

about the necessary offices in such government. Isaiah regards the people chosen by the Lord as a *polis*, and at the last day Jerusalem will be restored as a *polis* with all those appropriate officials.[2] Such preaching demands a knowledge of the world and of international events, as well as a profound grasp of the word of God as it speaks dynamically in changing times and in corporate terms.

That early Christian prophets spoke against a background of events in the world of the Roman Empire is also true, as a few references in Acts, like 11:27–30, and Revelation, can show. The seer of Patmos includes an impressive list of cargoes in which the merchants of the earth trafficked (Rev. 18:11–13), and he knew how shipmasters and sailors were intertwined with the commerce of the city of Babylon-Rome.

These ancient prophets spoke out of their often intense experiences with God and his will, in light of the Yahwistic (or Christian) traditions, and about current decisions, before they were made, during the decision-making, and in retrospect. Norman Gottwald concludes that in Israel they were "well-informed" about issues, as laymen of the day, neither utopian nor purely practical in their solutions, and that they tended to put things in the context of a plan (or the will) of God. Above all, win or lose on specific issues, they helped create a community which survived the fall of the states of Israel and Judah themselves. What Yahweh required towered over the wrecks of political empires, economic schemes, and social programs.

Is there anything analogous here to the call, in our time, for "persons skilled in ethical analysis" who can knowledgeably focus on "God's balance sheets" alongside corporations' financial statements and seek to factor in the human costs, environmental debits, and the moral elements of right, wrong, and shades of gray? Perhaps a prophetic ministry today must be waged in boardrooms and over coffee cups at committee meetings or late-night discussions in the bar (when *in vino veritas* may again prove

2. Gerhard von Rad, *Old Testament Theology*, 2 vols. (New York: Harper & Row, 1962), 2:150.

true). The corporation "cult centers" and "the marketplace" in the broadest sense become locales for asking after ethical concerns.

PEOPLE OF POWER, COME TO FAITH

It would be interesting to know how certain figures in the biblical accounts reacted with regard to their old corporate responsibilities after they came to faith or flirted with discipleship. We cannot usually tell, for the Scriptures are not biographies of such minor personages, any more than they are of Jesus.

The Old Testament narrates only rarely the conversion of an individual *goy* or the realization of faith in a lukewarm Israelite. Yet two characters deserve some mention here, if for no other reason than the ambiguity of their corporate responsibilities. First is Naaman, army commander in the Syrian forces. The account in 2 Kings 5 is a moving story about how the oral reporting of the "little people" brought a mighty man to healing and faith. Naaman was a man afflicted with leprosy, a disease which forced him—in spite of his power—to avoid close contact with other people and to be excluded from worship in the sanctuary of his God. An individual Israelite slave girl, carried off as a slave during a raid, told her mistress, Naaman's wife, that the prophet Elisha could cure the master's disease. When Naaman appeared in the court of Israel's king, Elisha sent word through a servant that the Syrian leader come to him. The prophet's instructions to Naaman that he should wash in the Jordan seven times in order to be healed were not well received, and so the commander left in a rage. His own servants urged him to return and wash in the river, and when he did, Naaman was indeed healed. It was the urging words of individual servants which led the mighty man to be made whole.

The Syrian commander's response was twofold. First, he requested two mounds of Israelite soil to take home so that he might offer sacrifices to no other god but the Lord. He had committed himself to the exclusive worship of the God who had healed him. Second, he asked Elisha that the Lord pardon him for something which would happen on his return home: When his own master, the king of Syria, would worship in the temple of the foreign god, Naaman would need to bow down too. While we have no way of knowing what changes—if any—took place in Naaman's leadership upon his return to his position of power, the tension within Naaman is instructive. Committed to the worship of one God, the Lord, he would be required by the worldly authority over him to bow down in another god's temple. Yet Naaman recognized clearly that such obedience conflicted with his own faith, and so he sought pardon in advance. While we might enjoy the story more if Naaman had refused to enter another god's temple, we can at least appreciate his awareness of the problem that the person of faith faces in the world of structure and power. Contemporary corporation heads who are Christians can surely understand his dilemma and at the same time learn from Naaman that the plans they execute are not necessarily good just because they are people of faith.

Solomon was perhaps the administrator par excellence in the Old Testament. We know little about the young man's life before he became king, and nothing about his faith or lack of faith in the Lord. Yet on coronation day Solomon became "the son of God" as the representative of that corporate body named Israel. He now had the power to make decisions which would be just and fair and good for all his people. He also had the ability to construct a glorious temple to the Lord, to build fortress towns for the protection of the kingdom, and to make trade alliances and economic treaties with other countries. He had enough wisdom to make concessions with regard to developing political forces, and he knew how to redistrict his kingdom for maximum efficiency. Under his leadership Israel became open to the world; art flourished, architecture reached new heights, and literature increased. It seemed to many that Solomon's reign was a "golden age."

But only to those who lived in Jerusalem were Solomon's achievements entirely positive. The rest of the kingdom really served to make Jerusalem a metropolis with its own set of laws and privileges. Elsewhere in the nation the population was subjected to forced labor (1 Kings 5:27) in order to achieve the aforementioned results. Jerusalem experienced all the benefits. And so, here is a story of a man of faith (see his prayer at 1 Kings 8:23–53) who had divine authority and sophisticated managerial skills but who used them for his own glory and for the welfare of a few over against the good of the whole community.

In the New Testament the ambiguity of the results of faith on corporate responsibility continues. Often all we have is the story of a call to discipleship or an illustrative anecdote to show what life in the early church could be like. For the Gospels and Acts, however, we do sometimes have a pattern where "mammon" (wealth, riches, the old way of doing worldly business) wins out over God's call; sometimes we have an account where God triumphs and genuine reform follows or the way of God's will is shown by specific deeds; sometimes the picture is a mixed, even confused one, of good and bad.

Aware of the dangers in possibly psychologizing texts not intended to be so treated, one might, nonetheless, want to ask how each of the following responded, and why.

	IN JESUS' MINISTRY	IN THE BOOK OF ACTS
Mammon over God	"The rich young ruler" (Mark 10:17–22, Matt. 19:16–22, Luke 18:18–23)	Ananias and Sapphira (5:1–11)
God over Mammon	Zaccheus (Luke 19:1–10)	Joseph Barnabas (4:36–37)
Mixed results	Judas (?)	Simon of Samaria (?) (8:13, 19–24)

Each of the first two cases may be meant by Luke as contrasting pairs. The very rich young man becomes sad at Jesus' demands; the little tax-collector from Jericho finds joy in giving half his goods to the poor and repaying fourfold those whom he had cheated. Barnabas follows through where Ananias and his wife selfishly held back for themselves what they had pledged.

Judas, of course, always remains an enigma, and Scripture itself offers several explanations for his actions (see Matt. 26:15; Luke 22:3; John 12:6 and 13:2).[3] But he was a disciple, and Matthew allows that he "repented," or at least rued what he had done (27:3ff.). Simon came to be regarded as a sorcerer and arch-heretic, but Luke says he believed and was baptized and repented of his villainy, upon Peter's stern words, "To hell with you and your money!" (Acts 8:20, Phillips). The last reference in Acts to him is seemingly a sincere request to Peter, "Pray for me."

In the gallery of saints and sinners, seeking to live God's will in a world of finance, power, and responsibility, one wonders how the proconsul in Cyprus, Sergius Paulus, reflected his new, astonished belief (Acts 13:6–12). What of the jailer at Philippi? Did his conversion, which led to such a tender scene of help-fulness to Paul and Silas (Acts 16:23–24, 27–34), spill over thereafter into the way he carried out his tasks in the machinery of Roman justice? There is also the tantalizing reference, in one of Paul's letters, to Erastus, a believer, who was also city treasurer (in Corinth? Rom. 16:23). One would love to know how these people introduced their new values into the structures of a non-Christian world in which they labored. We are not told, but we can think of them as forerunners for us, believers who were faced with applying faith to the daily round and the larger decisions of the corporate bodies of which they were a part.

BIBLICAL PRINCIPLES?

Are there themes, principles, or axioms in the Scriptures which God's people can apply in seeking to integrate ethical concerns with other elements that are an established part of decision-making?

(a) The demand for justice and truth, attested in the law of Sinai and elsewhere, is directed to all people, even those outside Israel for whom the will of God has been "written on the heart"

---

3. See also Bertil Gärtner, *Iscariot*, Facet Books (Philadelphia: Fortress Press, 1971).

(see Rom. 2:15). The dynamic nature of biblical law, however, prevents a simple application to the present or to any other situation. Law codes were constantly modernized, updated, and reinterpreted, even in the biblical period itself. For example, the book of the Covenant at Exodus 20:22–23:33 was modernized within the Old Testament period by the Code of Deuteronomy (Deuteronomy 12–26). The former code was the law of the premonarchical period, the time of the Judges (roughly 1200–1000 B.C.), and was directed to an agricultural society. The Deuteronomic code reinterpreted and expanded some of the same laws to meet a new sociological situation, one which under the influence of the monarchy had become more and more advanced in a monetary economy. Thus the particulars of laws, even biblical laws, constantly need to be examined in light of the needs of the community and the changing life of society.[4] Yet the divine demand for justice in any age and in every sociological setting is constant.

(b) Writ large throughout the Bible are the corporate nature of life and the interrelatedness of all things. No step is isolated from effects on others. The crassness of sin is precisely that one misdeed begets others, and the perpetrators become hardened in their own willfulness. On the other side, the possibility for blessing from God can be experienced by the whole community through an individual. Such indeed is the promise of God to Abraham (Gen. 12:1–3), which is effective for those in the Israelite community as well as for "all the families of the land." This blessing occurs for others through intercession (Gen. 18:22–33), through treaties (Gen. 26:28–31), through humble service (Gen. 39:1–5), even through suffering (Isa. 49:6), and ultimately through the death and resurrection of Christ (Gal. 3:8). The corporateness of sin and grace, of disaster and blessing, is consistent in the Bible even while individual responsibility is highlighted.

(c) There is the recognition that, while disciples are called to a "higher righteousness" in the kingdom, this is far from exempting

---

4. See the work by Richard L. Rohrbaugh, *The Biblical Interpreter: An Agrarian Bible in an Industrial Age* (Philadelphia: Fortress Press, 1978).

them from concern with "the world"; they are the more expected
to be salt and light for that world (Matt. 5:13–16). Hence,
believers have had laid upon them not only the "ethics of good
citizenship" (enlightened humanitarianism in corporate practices), as seen in the pastoral Epistles, the "tables of household
duties," or Romans 13, but also the extraordinary demands of the
kingdom, to set self aside (Luke 14:26), not to be dazzled by the
world in doing God's will (1 John 2:15–17), and to love not self
(or the company for which one works) above all else, but to love
others, neighbors and even enemies. The sovereign love-com-
mand, while addressed primarily to the community and for
the community, also looks beyond to become a factor in
"humanizing" our relations with the non-Christian world.[5] To
this extent, love for others becomes the most radical and
prophetic element for change in weighing many decisions.

(d) The same "corporate" aspect plays a vital part in the
believer's "support system" for injecting the ethical into decision-
making in big (or small) business. The believer-prophet-witness
to God's love and justice is no "lone ranger" but looks to the
church community for support, prayer, confirmation, and
correction of his own perceptions. All this encourages the
theologically and socially responsible Christian in a business
organization, lonely as he often feels, to stand at times apart from
and outside existing structures and to look at them both critically
and hopefully.

It is precisely this loneliness or solitude that often marks the life
of one called to play a prophetic role in society. Through
Jeremiah's faithful preaching of the Lord's word and will to the
power structures and the general populace of his day, the prophet
experienced isolation. He became an object of mockery (Jer.
20:7–8), persecution and suspicion (15:10–11, 15; 20:10), and
exclusion (15:17). In his witness the situation became so intense
that he complained to the Lord, "I *sat alone* because thy hand
was upon me." It seems that when the Lord elects spokespersons,

5. See Victor Paul Furnish, *The Love Command in the New Testament* (Nashville:
Abingdon Press, 1972), pp. 203, 211.

lonely individuals emerge in the midst of the social structures of order and comfort. This recognition leads to an affirmation of the individual's role in corporate life (see *b* above) and to an awareness that the dynamic will of God in changing situations (*a* above) throws the Lord's spokesperson into conflict with the prevailing mood and style of society. Thus it is divinely inspired courage which can make an individual emerge to speak on behalf of God to other individuals who run the corporations.

STARTING WHERE?

"Revive thy work, O Lord, beginning with me" (cf. Hab. 3:2) is a prayer, biblical in spirit. God's will can be asserted by any one of us, and, as Christopher Davis said earlier, ethical issues can be raised at all levels in a company. The Lord sometimes poses his questions to us from unexpected sources. But it is striking to note Davis's claim that the quality of leadership and the commitment of a company's top management are central factors in creating the environment where ethical issues are raised. "To whom much is given, much is required."

There was a time when Christianity seemed to make special efforts to enlist the decision-makers in a society. The New Testament already refers to some people in the lower echelons of government and business, as noted above. The next centuries record the church's attention to members of the imperial household and the conversion of socially significant persons. Mission endeavor has often started deliberately "at the top." Today we have a great number of corporation leaders who are at least nominally Christian, active in business, some of them practicing believers who puzzle over the "great divorce" between faith and the difficult and momentous decisions they must make so frequently. There exists, as it were, a Macedonian cry, "Come over here and help us."

Mission to and with such leaders is a modern enterprise in social-ethical evangelism which, for all its hazards and un-certainties, the church neglects at its peril and at the peril of the world. The goal is not any sort of "religious utopianism"

(Troeltsch) but "prophetic or pneumatic realism" (Elliger). Such realism, characteristic of the biblical prophets, enlightened by the Spirit of God, seeks to translate our relatedness to the living God as moral beings into a factor in the life-and-death decisions which the corporate world constantly makes. The ethical concern was emphatic in the Old Testament. Jesus' message to repent moved in the same direction. Paul's letters always stress the implications of our life in Christ for all we do.

If the corporation world is where the action is, that is where Christians, as God's spokespersons, must be too, with faith and knowledge and common sense, seeking to bring the Spirit and will of God to bear upon business realities.

BIBLIOGRAPHICAL SUGGESTIONS

Brueggemann, Walter. *The Prophetic Imagination.* Philadelphia: Fortress Press, 1978.

Fuller, Reginald H., ed. *Essays on the Love Commandment.* Philadelphia: Fortress Press, 1978.

Furnish, Victor Paul. *The Love Command in the New Testament.* Nashville: Abingdon Press, 1972. Especially pages 198–218.

Gärtner, Bertil. *Iscariot.* Facet Books Biblical Series. Philadelphia: Fortress Press, 1971.

Gese, Hartmut. "The Structure of the Decalogue." In *Fourth World Congress of Jewish Studies: Papers,* vol. 1. Jerusalem, 1967. Pages 155–59.

Gottwald, Norman K. *All the Kingdoms of the Earth: Israelite Prophecy and International Relations in the Ancient Near East.* New York: Harper & Row, 1964. Especially pages 350–92; summarizes views of Troeltsch, Elliger, and others.

Harrelson, Walter. *The Ten Commandments and Human Rights.* Overtures to Biblical Theology. Philadelphia: Fortress Press, forthcoming.

Hengel, Martin. *Property and Riches in the Early Church.* Translated by John Bowden. Philadelphia: Fortress Press, 1974.

The Interpreter's Dictionary of the Bible. Edited by G. A. Buttrick et al. Nashville: Abingdon Press, 1962. See the articles "Trade and Commerce" by G. A. Barrois, vol. 4, pp. 677–83, esp. pp. 679ff; and "Tax Collector" by B. J. Bamberger, vol. 4, pp. 522–23.

Robinson, H. Wheeler. *Corporate Personality in Ancient Israel.* 1964. Reprint. Philadelphia: Fortress Press, 1980.

Rohrbaugh, Richard L. *The Biblical Interpreter: An Agrarian Bible in an Industrial Age.* Philadelphia: Fortress Press, 1978.

Wendland, Heinz-Dietrich. *Die Kirche in der modernen Gesellschaft.* Darmstadt: Wissenschaftliche Buchgesellschaft, 1973. Pages 38–62, on proclamation and social order in the New Testament.

Wolff, Hans Walter. *Anthropology of the Old Testament.* Translated by Margaret Kohl. Philadelphia: Fortress Press, 1974. Especially the chapter "The Individual and the Community," pages 214–22.

Corporate Social Responsibility: Sources of Authority

George W. Forell

OUR society is based on the availability of expert counsel to help us solve every kind of problem. We rely on a variety of authorities to assist us when we need advice. If you have pains in your chest you will probably go to a physician for an evaluation of your condition and competent medical recommendations. If your automobile does not run well you will take it to a garage and request a skilled appraisal by a mechanic. If you want to travel abroad you will presumably go to a travel agent to obtain authoritative information. In general, we know where to turn for help in the many and varied situations that challenge us in life.

But in the introductory essay of this volume the author makes it clear that such authoritative counsel is not available to executives of the large business corporations who are confronted with complex ethical decisions. While they are able to obtain expert advice on legal and financial questions, similarly competent counsel where questions of social and moral responsibility are involved is hard to find and may not even be sought.

This is a matter of considerable concern to everybody, since our life is affected in innumerable important ways by corporations and the way they meet their social responsibilities. Most of the products we buy, from the food at the supermarket to the car we drive to work and the gasoline we use to fuel it, are manufactured, transported, and sold by corporations. But it is not only those products we obviously consume, like food and fuel, that are produced by corporations. We may live in an apartment house owned by a corporation, or travel in a bus or airplane leased by a corporation to a corporation. We may be employed by corporations, from the multinational "megacorporations" earning billions of dollars each year to the "nonprofit corporations" which employ pastors and many teachers, nurses, and social workers. In spite of their obvious differences, these latter corporations deserve our attention as well, since in our society the behavior of the megacorporations is quickly imitated and adapted by the charitable corporations in which we worship, learn, and exercise our private charities. It has been frequently observed that the meetings of a national church body show greater similarity to the stockholders' meeting of a corporation than to the apostolic council in Jerusalem described in the Acts of the Apostles. The same anonymity of actual decision-making characterizes both.

Because of the ubiquity and power of corporations, the question of whether they should be socially responsible is a matter of overwhelming importance to our society. As far as business corporations are concerned, the matter has been addressed and to an extent solved by a redefinition of the original purposes of a business corporation by the courts. The traditional legal view of what such a corporation should do was expressed by a Michigan court in 1919 when it held:

> A business corporation is organized and carried on primarily for the benefit of the stockholders. . . . It is not within the lawful power of a board of directors to shape and conduct the affairs of a corporation for the merely incidental benefit of shareholders and for the primary purpose of benefiting others.[1]

The court's opinion stated explicitly that a corporation had no right to use its resources to benefit anyone other than the stockholders, in other words, that it was not allowed to make social responsibility its primary objective.

But this traditional view has since been abandoned by the courts, and "benefit" has been transformed into a legal fiction.

---

1. *Dodge* v. *Ford Motor Co.*, as quoted in Philip I. Blumberg, *The Megacorporation in American Society* (Englewood Cliffs, N.J.: Prentice-Hall, 1975), p. 6.

Thus, in 1953, a small New Jersey corporation whose executives wanted to contribute corporate funds to Princeton University was allowed to do so; the court held that such a contribution would indirectly contribute to the "free enterprise system" and the availability of college-trained persons for managerial positions.[2] Indeed, as early as 1864 an English court had ruled that an insurance company could honor claims of eighty-one Liverpool policyholders arising from an explosion, although the policies expressly excluded explosion risks, because such action would advance the insurance company's interests in the long run and thus be good for business. In other words, it was decided that something could be in the long run advantageous for a corporation even though in the short run it might prove expensive. Social responsibility was justified if it could be shown to be in the long-term interest of the corporation and its stockholders.

But in a 1972 decision a court abandoned even the fiction of the long-term stockholder interest. Here the effort on the part of a Denver newspaper to reject a takeover bid—clearly advantageous to the stockholders—was allowed. The takeover would have ended local control of the particular newspaper. In siding with the directors' rejection of the financially beneficial bid the court said:

> In this case we have a corporation engaged chiefly in the publication of a large metropolitan newspaper whose obligation and duty is something more than the making of corporate profits. Its obligation is threefold: to the stockholders, to the employees, and to the public.[3]

The way was now clear for corporations to exhibit social responsibility, but only when they desire to do so. The initiative for expressing social responsibility rested entirely with the corporation, or more precisely with its executives. It was unlikely that this option would always be exercised, because many people still believed that any expression of social responsibility on the

2. Ibid., p. 7.
3. *Herald Co.* v. *Seawell*, ibid., p. 9.

part of a business corporation is both ill-advised and ultimately counterproductive.

The well-known American economist Milton Friedman recently stated:

> The view has been gaining widespread acceptance that corporate officials and labor-leaders have a "social responsibility" that goes beyond serving the interests of their stockholders or their members. This view shows a fundamental misconception of the character and nature of a free economy. In such an economy there is one and only one social responsibility of business—to use its resources and engage in activities designed to increase its profits so long as it stays within the rules of the game which is to say, engaged in open and free competition without deception or fraud.[4]

Not only is the consideration of "social responsibility" not compelling, but it is actually said to "thoroughly undermine the very foundations of our free society." It is "a fundamentally subversive doctrine," for, "if businessmen do have a social responsibility other than making maximum profits for stockholders, how are they to know what it is?"[5] The authority for these words is Friedman's frequently quoted and apparently inerrant scripture, Adam Smith, *The Wealth of Nations* (1776; book 4, chap. 2), where we learn that the individual in pursuing his own interest is "led by an invisible hand to promote an end which was no part of his intention. Nor is it always the worse for the society that it was no part of it. By pursuing his own interest, he frequently promotes that of the society more effectually than when he really intends to promote it." Smith added, not entirely without producing a favorable response in most modern readers, "I have never known much good done by those affected to trade for the public good."

Thus the concern for corporate public responsibility is not only questionable but in the opinion of this eminent economist clearly dangerous. The reason Friedman gives is also significant. How does the corporation executive know what his social responsibility

4. As quoted in Edwin Mansfield, *Monopoly Power and Economic Performance* (New York: W. W. Norton Co., 1978), pp. 122–23.
5. Ibid., p. 122.

is? There are no clear guidelines; he hears no voice from Mount Sinai. Even if he were eager to carry out the "will of the Lord," how would he discover what this will is?

The same question must also be raised in connection with the judge's decision quoted earlier, that a corporation has a threefold obligation: to the stockholders, to the employees, and to the public. The obligation to the stockholders, to make as much money as possible, is definable and measurable. The obligation to the employee, to maintain his job and to pay him as much money as possible, is also definable and measurable, even though it may be at odds with the first obligation. But compared to these two, the obligation to the public seems as vague as the very notion of "the public" and may very well reduce itself to the opinion of the judge: the public interest is what the judge says is the public interest. Is the judge the expert who is able to decide what the moral responsibility of a corporation is? Indeed, this seems increasingly to be the case. Judges decide who may be born and who shall be aborted, who may live and who must die. Compared to these godlike decisions, the definition of the social responsibility of a corporation may seem almost trivial. But the mere *fact* that judges make such decisions and that everything from the sublime questions of life and death to the comparatively petty issue of admission to a college of nursing or even the grade a student receives in a course at the university is being litigated hardly makes this situation desirable. Is there another way to establish criteria for the social responsibility of corporations besides the "invisible hand" of Adam Smith and Milton Friedman or the idiosyncratic opinions of the courts?

If one turns in this dilemma to the religious communities for their advice, one is not immediately impressed that an adequate alternative to the "invisible hand" or the "infallible judiciary" has been provided. In a recent issue of *The Cresset* (February 1979), Harold A. Gram listed the types of approaches taken by churches to encourage social responsibility in corporations:

1. Attempts to change the behavior, attitudes, values, goals and ethics of business managers as individual Christians operating within a business environment.

2. Statements and expressions of concern proposing ideal behavior for business managers, corporations and society as a whole. These statements of policy take various forms and shapes . . . . Desired behavior and policy statements on business social goals are communicated by denominations and groups or by direct communication with the corporation.

3. Encouragement and support are provided by churches to concerned citizens, endowment fund managers, and others, to express their concerns and values within the corporate environment as active shareholders or as "outside directors." Shareholders are encouraged to ask questions about corporate social policy and corporate behavior and even to participate in proxy fights . . . .

4. Churches have supported various types of sanctions including boycotts of various products and companies. "Sanctions" have included the refusal to buy certain products or refusal to invest in certain bonds or shares.

5. The Corporate Information Center of the National Council of Churches is developing a social aspect index, which they believe will be used along with Dun and Bradstreet ratings. The social aspect index will assist investors and others in rating a company as a social as well as a financial investment.

This is an impressive and fairly comprehensive list. Gram claims, however, that these efforts have proven largely ineffective, since religious groups tend to underestimate the complexity of the corporation and of the decision-making process. And religious groups tend to view the process of decision-making too individualistically, unaware of the "constrained social, economic and political environment" of the decision-maker. But while this criticism is certainly true of some of the approaches listed above, others are conscious efforts to change the social, economic, and political environment—often with little or no result.

To bring some order into the confusion concerning the varied sources of authority so far described, it may be useful to recall the old theological distinction between "law" and "gospel." Law is the principle and operation of order in the world, and Christians have held in agreement with most other major religious traditions that all human beings everywhere and at all times are under the law. It is not necessary to hold any particular religious views in order to be addressed by the law, for the law is found in the statutes of the religions of the human race as well as in the reasoning of the philosophers. For those who do not have access to or do not trust the codes of the great religious traditions, the law is available through the light of nature or conscience. As Paul stated in Rom. 2:14-15, "When Gentiles who do not possess the law carry out its precepts by the light of nature, then, although they have no law, they are their own law, for they display the effect of the law inscribed in their hearts" (NEB).

What the advocates of this view have to offer as source of authority is the reasonable application of a basic human insight such as "Do unto others as you would like them to do unto you." The universality and plausibility of this insight in its simple and sophisticated expressions, ranging from the so-called silver or golden rule to Kant's categorical imperative, is a matter of record. It is recognized as valid even by people who have no intention of obeying it. It operates with certain hidden assumptions which must be stated and explained. For example, the "other" these rules talk about is seen differently in different cultures. In the tradition of Paul and the Hellenistic world, the "other" was every human being regardless of race or class. This was as obvious to Paul as it was to the Stoic philosophers of his time, and it made the basics of Christian ethics plausible to a world which found Christian theology highly implausible. In its Western version, this basic "law" does not include animals, and even the position of women and children was at first somewhat ambiguous. The status of the unborn child under this law is one of the major moral dilemmas of our time.

Because "law" as here defined depends not on "religion" but only on reason and evidence, it has broad cross-cultural appeal. Even people who go against this "law" feel compelled to defend their actions in its terms, giving hypocritical lip service to goodness even as they pursue evil. Thus, in the words of La Rochefoucauld, "Hypocrisy is the homage that vice pays to virtue."

While this "law" is admittedly vague and not easy to define in a specific situation, "social responsibility" is precisely the pursuit of this "law" with all the intellectual and moral resources available to the human race. Far from denigrating this secular search for justice, it is important for the religious community to take advantage of this universal sense of right and wrong and the pervasive conviction that right both exists and ought to be pursued, in order to build concern for these realities into the structures of our society, including corporations and the rules governing them.

There is no easily available "source of authority," but for those willing to search for definable criteria of social responsibility, the effort is eminently worthwhile. It demands the cooperation of people who have heretofore frequently ignored or even despised each other, the "thinkers" and the "doers." The conflict between so-called "eggheads" and men and women of action is particularly marked in America. More than a century ago Alexis de Tocqueville observed:

> I think that in no country in the civilized world is less attention paid to philosophy than in the United States. . . . To evade the bondage of system and habit, of family maxims, class opinions, and, in some degree, of national prejudices; to accept tradition only as a means of information, and existing facts only as a lesson to be used in doing otherwise and doing better; to seek the reason of things for oneself, and in oneself alone; to tend to results without being bound to means, and to strike through the form to the substance—such are the principal characteristics of . . . the philosophical method of the Americans.[6]

As a result of this attitude, both so-called conservatives in defense of corporations and so-called radicals in their attacks have generally avoided the challenge Christopher Davis presents in the introductory essay of this volume when he suggests: "As efforts by business persons to take ethical issues into account expand, one can hope that there will also be increased attention to this area by persons skilled in ethical analysis." Ethical analysis is possible and relevant, but it must be serious and well-informed. It would appear to be one of the tasks of the Christian church as a

6. Alexis de Tocqueville as quoted by E. Enberg, *On Civilizing the Corporation* (Santa Barbara, Calif.: Capra Press, 1976), p. 45.

communion of people who have a vast variety of talents to furnish the occasion and the forum for men and women concerned about the future, so profoundly affected by corporations, to meet and offer suggestions that might increase social responsibility. It is likely that a large number, if not a majority, of corporation executives in the United States and Canada are members of religious communities. They are used by institutional religion for fund-raising drives and for aid in the administration of the religious organization and its various institutions. They may even teach occasionally in the schools of the churches. Their special "talents" in guiding the churches into a more subtle understanding of the corporations and in finding roads to social responsibility are largely ignored. When professional religionists talk to them as professional corporation executives, they tend to treat them either with kid gloves and an attitude of veneration because of the money they have or control, or beat them over the head with abandon as specimens of evil robber barons who deserve only castigation for the many and obvious failures of their organizations. In the light of the Davis essay, both attitudes are beside the point. Only people familiar with the structure and operation of corporations are in a position to offer helpful suggestions to guide these agencies in the direction of greater social responsibility. The access of religious communities in the West to such people is an opportunity they should not waste with ill-informed rhetoric.

Not that such ill-informed rhetoric has been a problem only of the religionists. As recently as 1970, Henry Ford, when asked if he thought the Episcopal Church was justified in praying for General Motors to leave South Africa, replied, "I don't think it's any of their goddamn business. It's none of our business how South Africans run themselves."[7]

But by and large, as David Vogel[8] has pointed out, the concern of citizens has affected the corporations and occasionally moved them to confront issues before they were forced to do so by public

7. As quoted in David Vogel, *Lobbying the Corporation* (New York: Basic Books, 1978), p. 203.
8. Ibid.

opinion or the courts. "Citizens' challenges have helped to increase the visibility and public scrutiny of corporate decisions. The business corporation is far less of an abstraction than it was a decade ago. . . . The most fundamental contribution of citizen pressures has been to link corporations more closely with the vitality and turbulence of the democratic process."[9]

The task of the Christian church in this process is to bear witness to the reality of the divine law, reflected, inadequately to be sure, in the perception of natural law as defined by philosophers and theologians through the ages. In this way the pervasive moral relativism that plagues our age and identifies the will of God with business success competitively achieved may be gradually overcome. It might also restrain the equally deadly legal positivism which identifies the decision of the judge with the divine law. If left unchecked, and if the judiciary falls captive to some pervasive ideology, positivism can lead to the horrors of some form of fascism, as exemplified by Nazi courts with their slogan "Recht ist was dem Volke nützt" (Law is what is useful to the *Volk*).

In its witness against relativism, the Christian community may count on the support of a large array of men and women of goodwill who are equally committed to the goal of greater social responsibility. At the same time, the Christian church must proclaim the gospel of God's love and forgiveness, which will enable those who accept it to participate gladly and courageously in the above-mentioned task. While the gospel does not supply the answers that research and reason must provide, it enables those who trust it to persevere in spite of the discouragements and failures that are bound to plague this pursuit. In the light of the gospel, the polarization between the human opponents in the debate over corporate social responsibility may be significantly reduced. This conflict is not Armageddon, the battle between God and the demons, but rather a very important human conflict in which the diabolization of the opponent contributes nothing to the achievement of a desirable solution. As biblical religion

9. Ibid., pp. 226, 227.

demythologized the powers of nature which were worshiped by the neighbors of the Hebrews, so the gospel should help to "demythologize" the ideological demons—economic, political, and social—which make a humane approach to our problems of social responsibility so difficult. The "invisible hand" is as real a demon as "Baal" in the Old Testament, and worshiping the ideology of legal positivism is as destructive as the worship of mammon. In its opposition to idolatry, the biblical faith can supply us with important insights into the polymorphous idolatries of our time.

Many years ago Augustine observed that avarice is not a defect of gold but a defect of the person who misguidedly loves gold and thus deserts righteousness, which should be immeasurably preferred to gold.[10] We could say with equal justification that the social irresponsibility of corporations is not so much the result of the existence of corporations but a defect of the men and women who have worshiped a golden calf. Such idolatry permitted the development of a social, economic, and political environment in which "the compounded concentration of economic power and control threaten the primacy of political decision-making by democratic institutions and the maintenance of social and political controls over the major centers of power, which are essential components of a free democratic society."[11]

In view of this danger the religious communities, in cooperation with other men and women desiring greater social justice, should carefully and persistently work in the direction of greater corporate social responsibility. The situation seems far from hopeless, as William Withers observed after surveying the field in his book *The Corporation and Social Change*. He noted:

> Over the last one hundred and fifty years businesses and large corporations especially, have changed from purely individualistic enterprises to semi-public institutions with great social responsibilities. Their responsibilities have enlarged in recent years to include protection of the physical environment and aid to the disadvantaged. Very encouraging is the willingness of businesses

10. Augustine *City of God* 14. 6.
11. Blumberg, *The Megacorporation in American Society*, p. 177.

to assume these new responsibilities despite the costs involved
. . . . To be sure, in many instances businesses had to be forced by
law to accept their growing obligations, especially to consumers.
But the trend toward greater awareness of social needs is strong
and justifies considerable optimism.[12]

While this may be too euphoric a view, we should realize what
Peter F. Drucker said more than a decade ago:

> The large-scale organization of business enterprise is very new. It is
> therefore highly probable that we are not very good as yet in
> organizing and managing this social institution. That it has great
> potential has already been proved. The realization of this potential
> demands hard work on problems of order and structure, in-
> dividual self-development and community values and beliefs. It
> demands above all that our large corporations and their managers
> take the largest view of their functions and make the greatest
> demands upon themselves.[13]

Others besides business people, indeed all who have an interest
in the future of the human race, must try to help in this process.
The Christian community should try to make available its particular insights and thus become one, though not the only,
significant source of authority for the corporation which will be
for the foreseeable future an inescapable and pervasive power
structure in the Western world.

12. William Withers, *The Corporations and Social Change* (Woodbury, N.Y.: Barron's Educational Series, Inc., 1972), p. 112.
13. Peter F. Drucker, *The Concept of the Corporation* (New York: New American Library, 1964), p. 247.